This project is dedicated to the voiceless children in the world today. May you be restored, find your purpose, and use your voice to change your sphere of influence!

Copyright ©2013 Emily S. Russell

All rights reserved. No part of this publication may be reproduced, stored in a retrieval system or transmitted in any form, or by any means, electronic, mechanical, recorded, photocopied or otherwise, without the prior permission of the copyright owner, except by a review of who may quote passages in a review.

Emily S. Russell is the author and illustrator of this book. All other songs were composed by her with the exception of "I'm Special", which was composed by George W. Russell, Jr.

Printed version created in the United States of America by Emily S. Russell.

FOREWORD

As a pediatrician and school volunteer, often I'm asked to visit classrooms to inspire students in their academic pursuits. I open by encouraging them to identify and celebrate their innate gifts and talents.

"If you're a great reader," I prompt, "raise your hand." "Let's see the excellent writers, the strong athletes, the curious scientists. Raise your hands high if you're a math whiz or an outstanding singer!"

What a stark difference in the responses of the early-grade learners compared to those of the later grades! Enthusiastic first- and second-graders can do all that and more. They're intellectual giants, musical geniuses, and future Olympians. Their artwork, they proudly announce, is already on exhibit in the gallery on their home refrigerators and the walls of their grandparents' offices.

The fifth- and six-graders, on the other hand, are far more tentative. Their raised hands are fewer in number, slower-moving, and not nearly as high. What happened in the interim? Who killed their promise? What stole their hope? Who destroyed their vision? As a pediatrician and minister, I struggle to find ways to ensure that our children's confidence in God's gifts remains strong throughout their school years and beyond. Given the abundance of confidence-busting weapons that bombard them, I long for compelling sources with positive messages that counter the prevailing doom.

Into this gap of time and spaces steps my exceptional writer-, artist-, and musician-friend, Emily Russell, with *Destiny, Purpose, & Plans for Me*. For more than 25 years, Emily has created visual and musical works of art as ready sources of hope and healing. Ignited by her passion for God and heart for God's children, Emily has produced a masterful book and songs with captivating images and powerful affirmations. *Destiny, Purpose, & Plans for Me* is an urgent counterpoint to the constant communication of low expectations that chip away at the determination of too many children to walk toward their destiny.

Indeed, *Destiny, Purpose & Plans for Me* isn't just another children's book; it's an experience that will inspire both children and adults to hold fast to God's promises, to raise their hands high and in a hurry to claim their hope and future.

Rev. Gloria E. White-Hammond, M.D.

Co-Pastor, Bethel AME Church
Retired Pediatrician, South End Community Health Center

PREFACE

This book was birthed out of songs I composed for Vacation Bible School where the theme was about finding your purpose in life and walking in destiny. As my husband and I recorded those songs with an incredible group of singers and musicians, images of children's faces flooded my mind. It was the children of the world calling for love and purpose! I combined the lyrics of the songs with eighteen painted portraits of children from various backgrounds and ethnicities. And that became *Destiny, Purpose & Plans For Me*.

I am very passionate about children feeling loved and knowing that have value, simply because they are who they are. It is also my prayer that children who are voiceless and overlooked find their worthiness and uniqueness through the pages of this book.

By reading this book and listening to the accompanying songs, anyone can gain a clearer understanding that you were designed with a unique set of gifts and abilities. You are, indeed, special, and worthy of greatness!

Parents and guardians, you can use this book during reading time with your child.

Teachers and therapists, this material can be implemented in any learning environment, recovery group, or youth group setting.

The esteem-building vocabulary page in the back of the book can be discussed and used through creative writing, theater, art, dance, and song... any form of self-expression that encourages children and youth to share their thoughts, fears, hopes, and dreams.

I want thank my family for all the support you gave as I worked on and completed this project. To my husband, George W. Russell, Jr., the co-producer of the album and composer of the song "I'm Special." To the Kickstarter Patrons who helped make this project successful…Thank You!

Thank YOU, dear reader, for taking a chance on this life-changing art & musical experience!

Emily S. Russell

DESTINY, PURPOSE

& PLANS FOR ME!

Emily S. Russell

I'm on my way to being

what you have made me to be.

It's not really clear right now,

but I see SIGNS along the way!

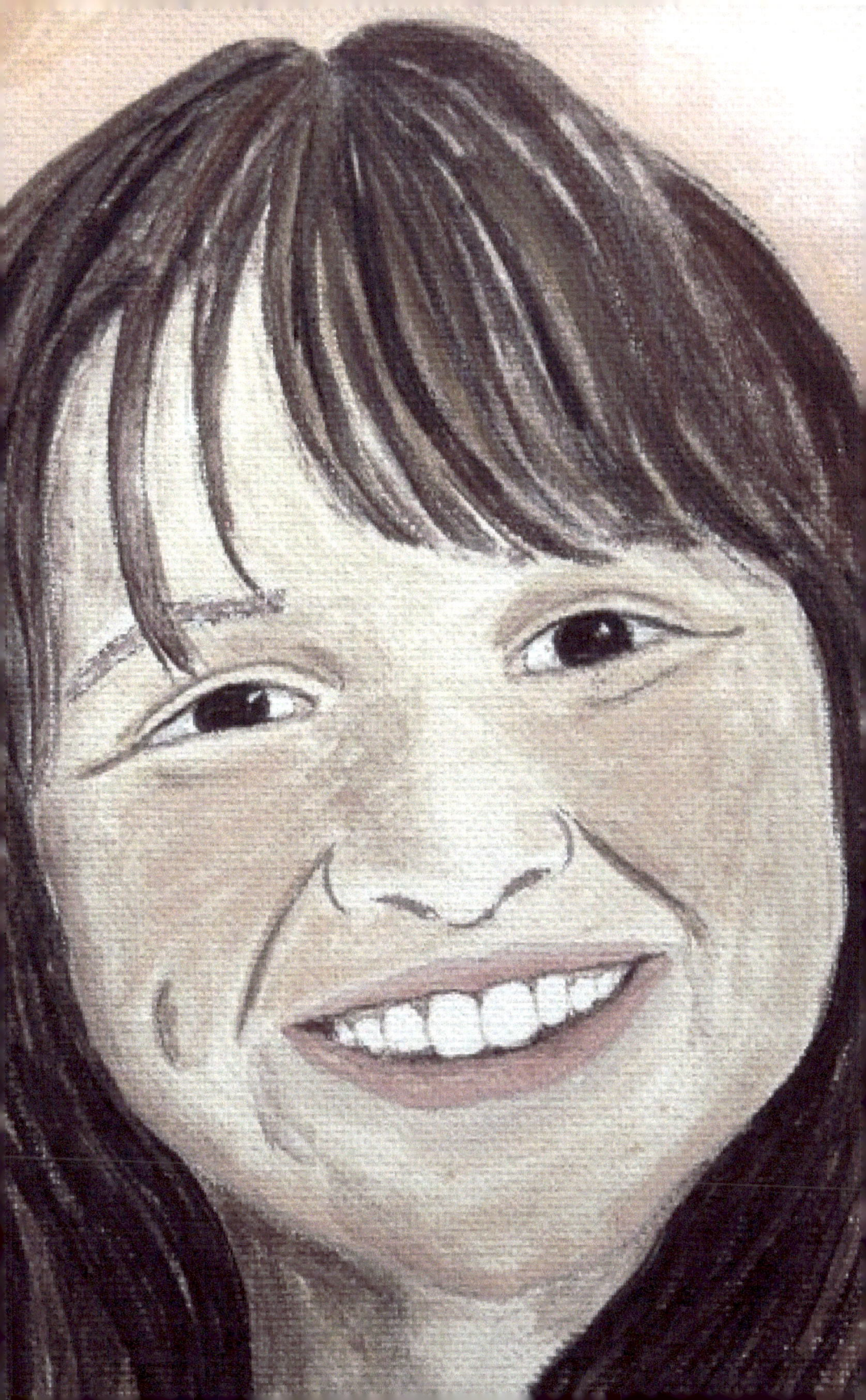

Mother, father, friends, and family,

telling me to be all I can be.

You have given me purpose,

and I'm DETERMINED to walk in my destiny!

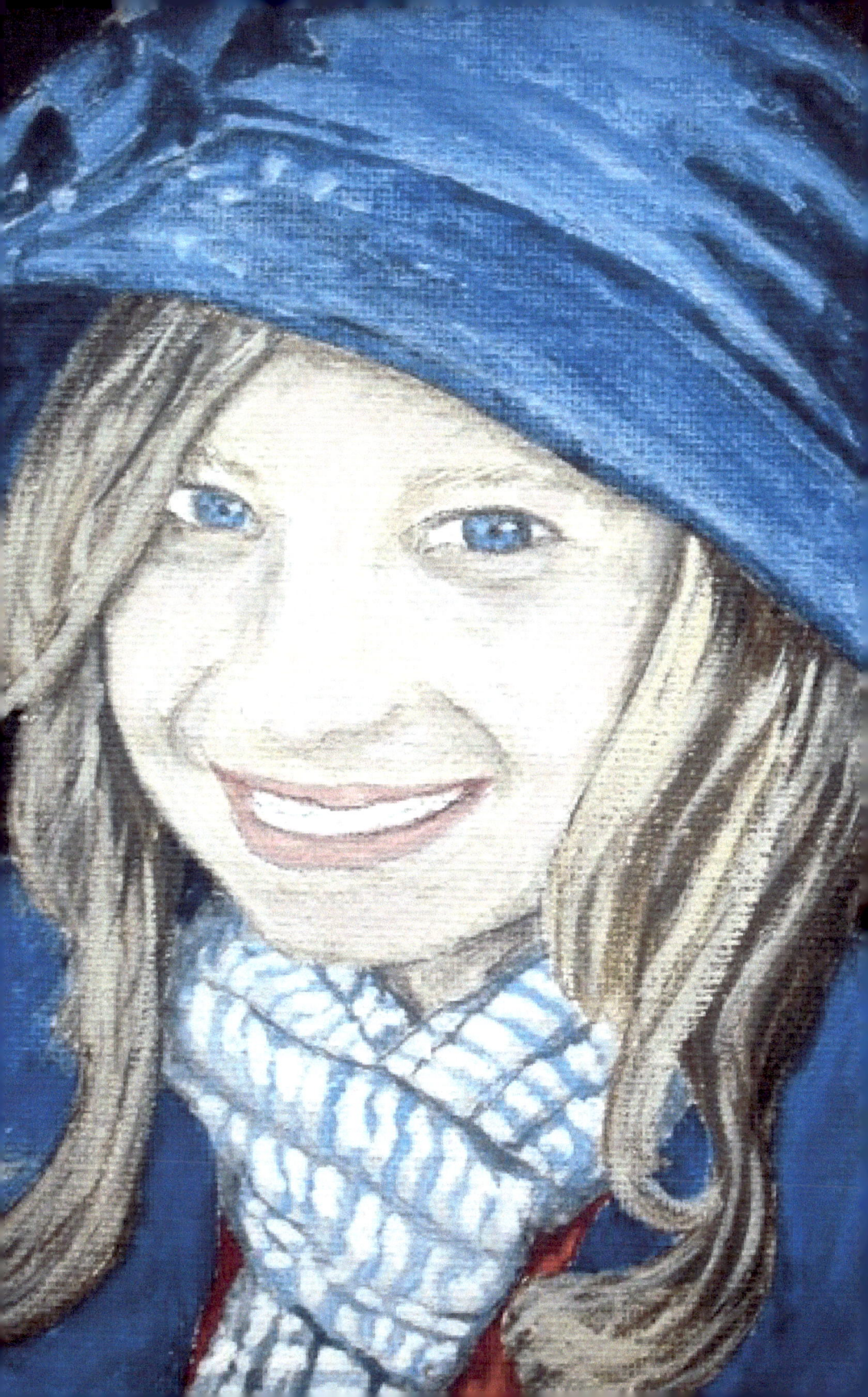

You have plans for me! Plans to PROSPER me!

To give me hope and a future.

You have given me purpose,

and I'm determined to walk in my destiny!

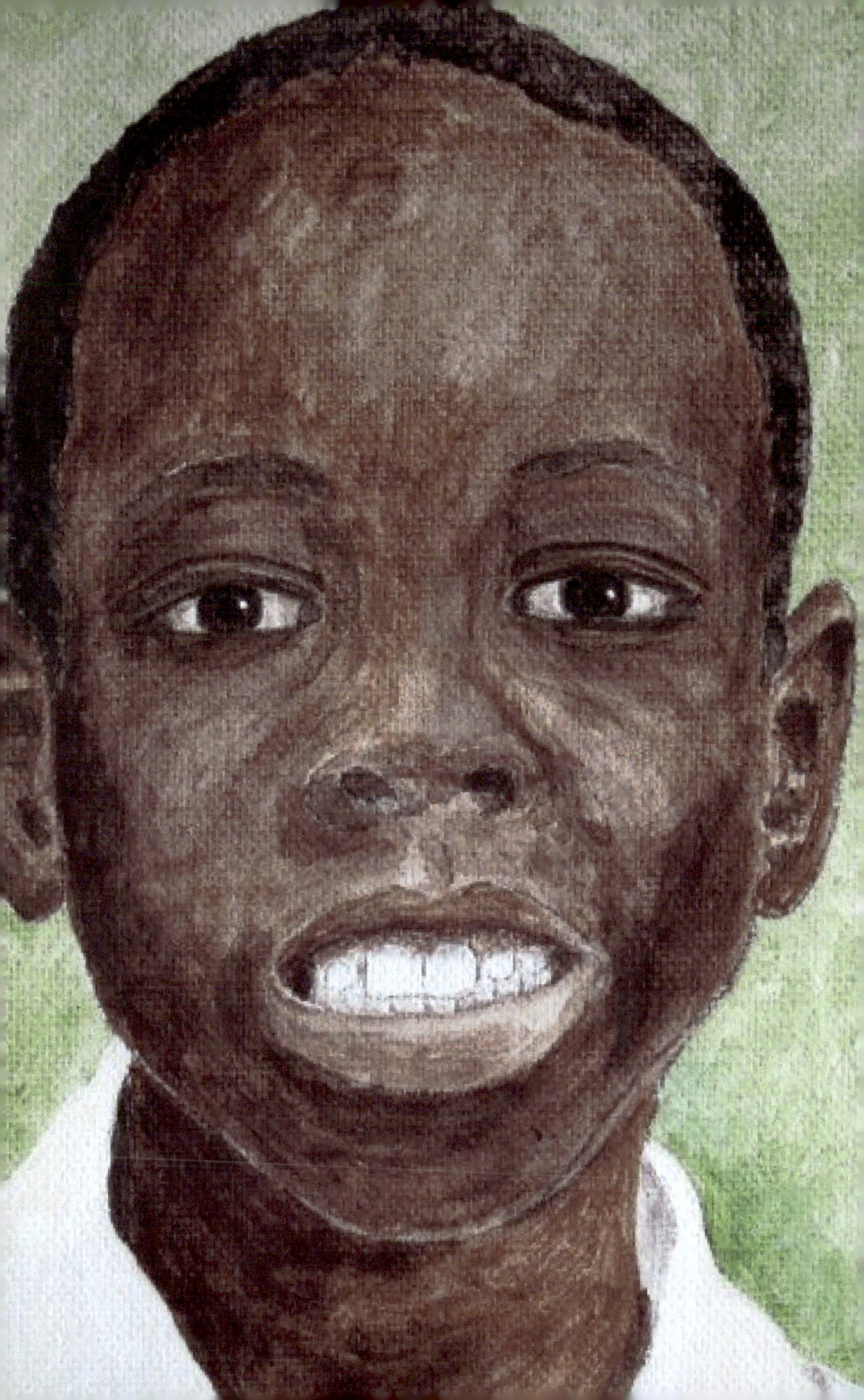

You DESIGNED me for your purpose.

Everything about me is UNIQUE!

You designed me for your purpose.

That is why I can sing!

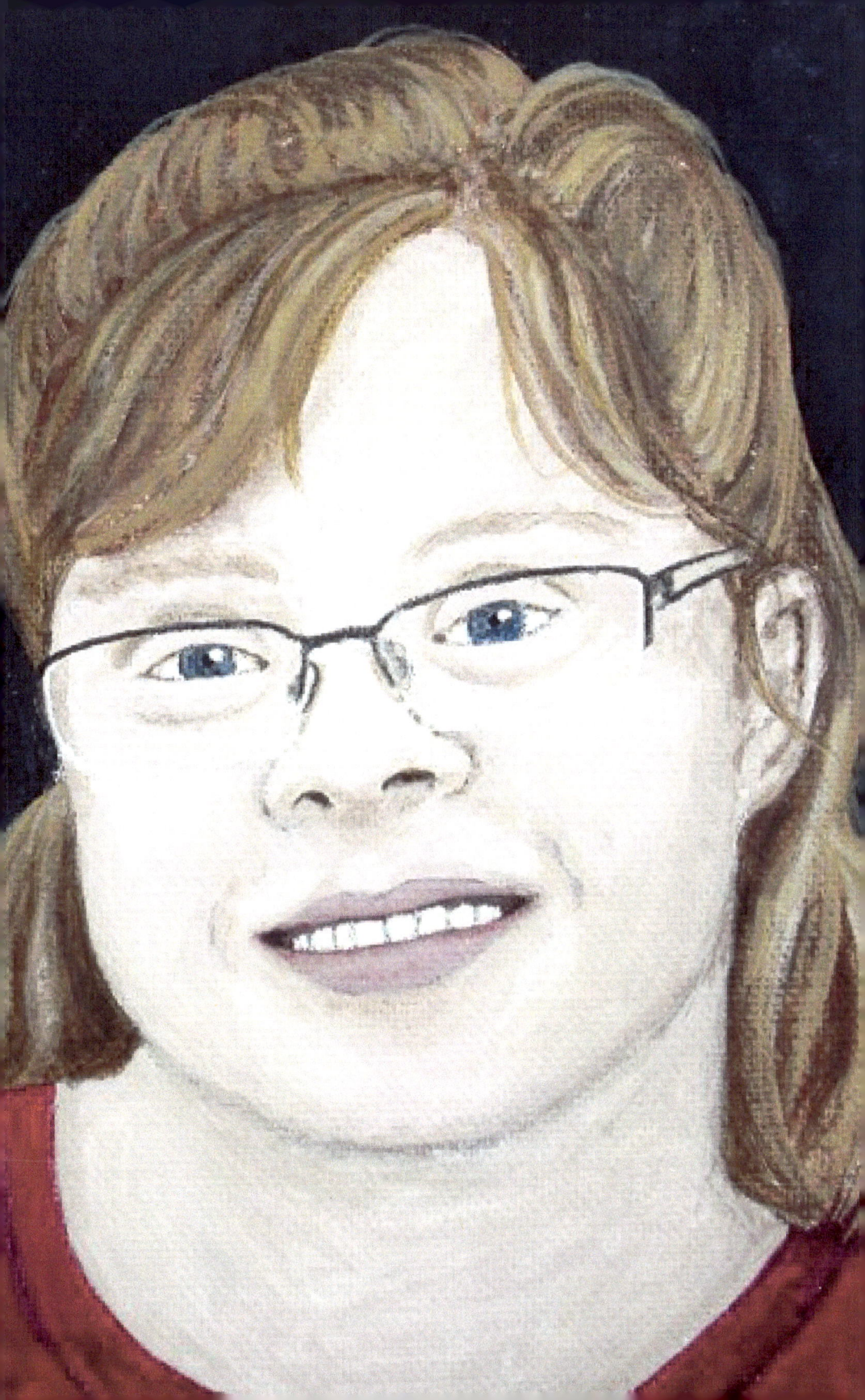

My designer, My CREATOR,

My designer... I worship you!

I am fearfully and

WONDERFULLY MADE!

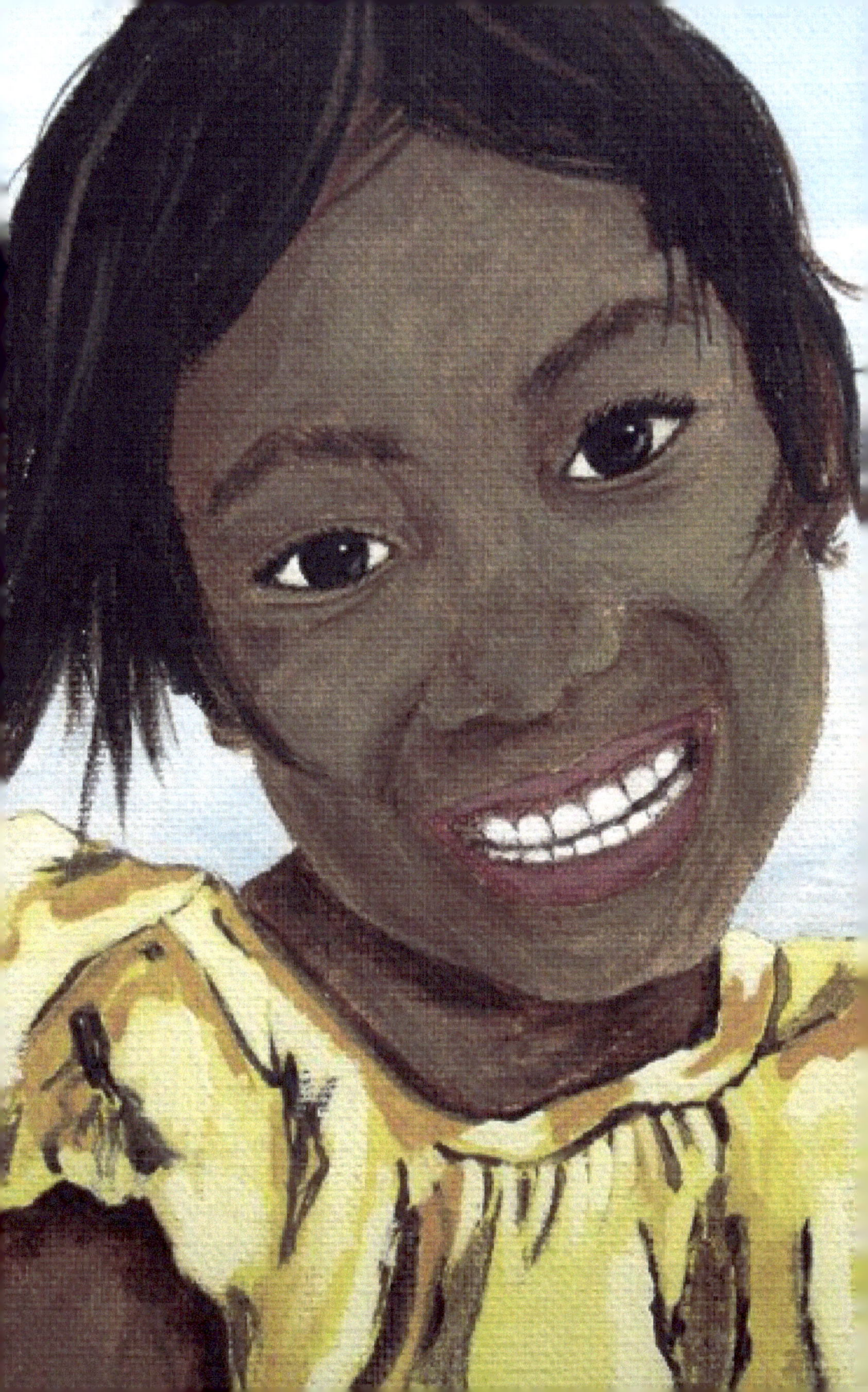

DESTINY, destiny...

I'm gonna walk in my destiny!

Got to be sure of my destiny!

You need to be sure of your destiny!

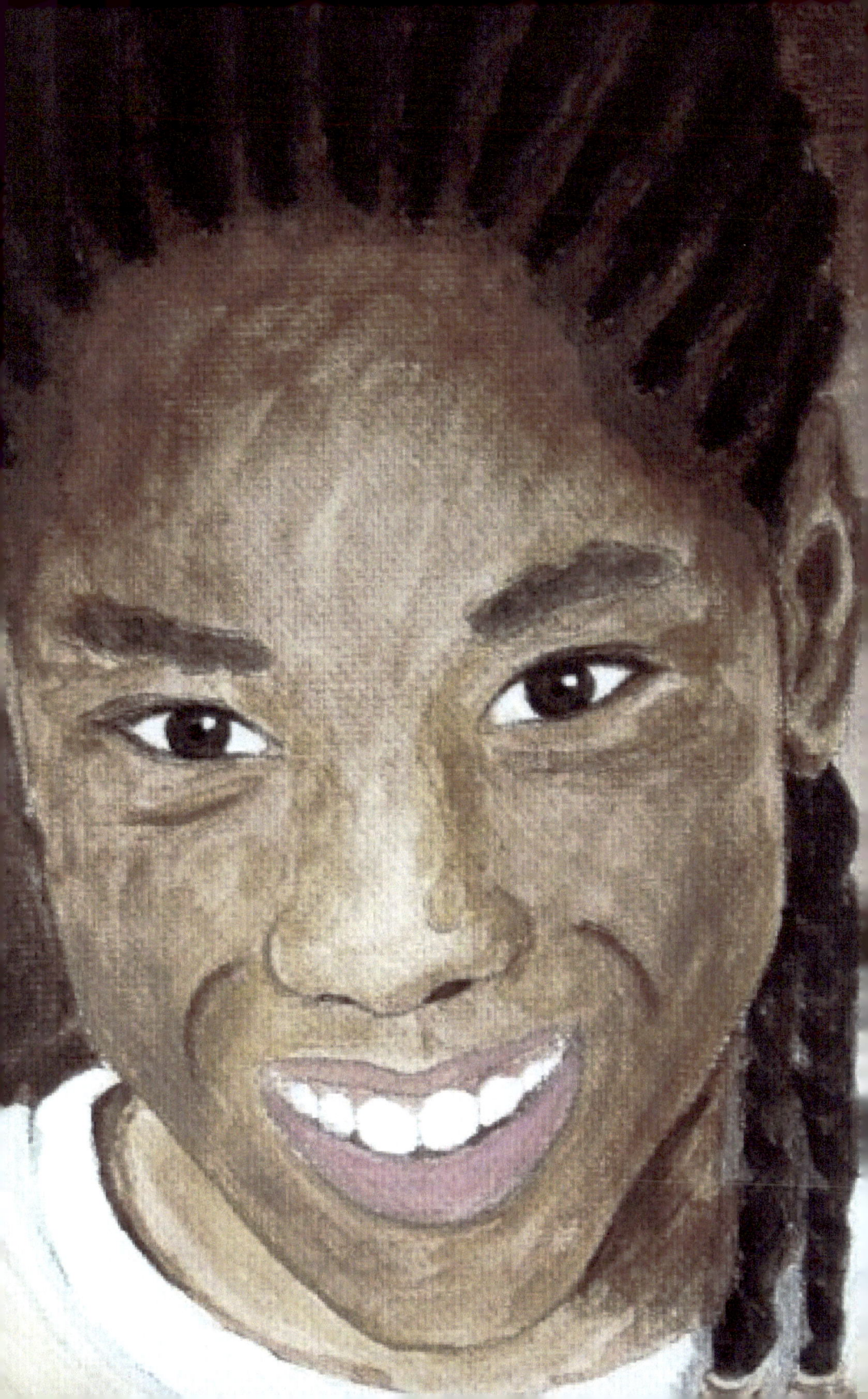

I'm destined to be all that God wants me to be.

I know God's purpose will PREVAIL.

Nothing can stop me

from my destiny!

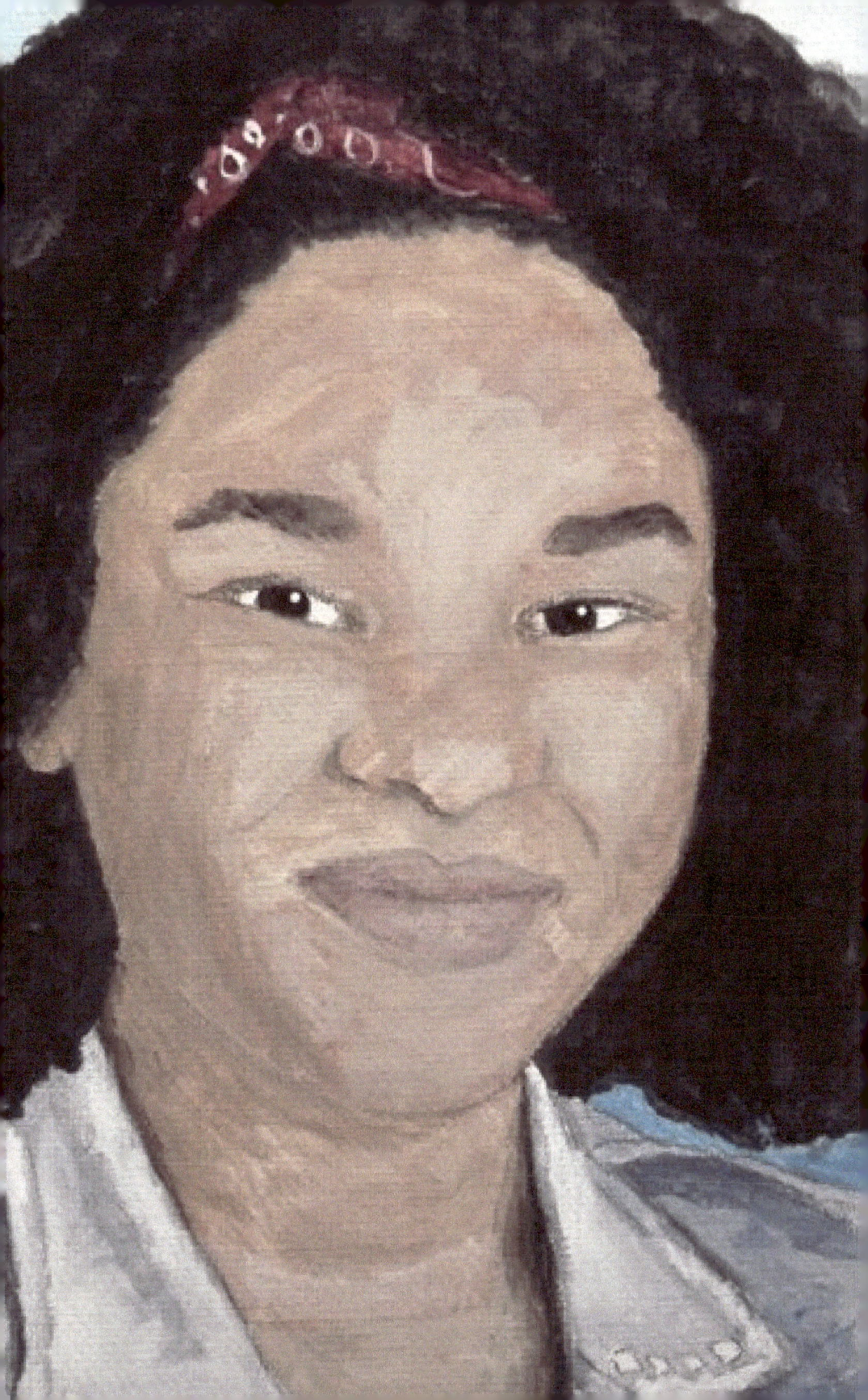

Some say I am TOO YOUNG to understand.

Some say I haven't lived long enough to see.

But you used a boy with bread and fishes,

and I know that you can use me!

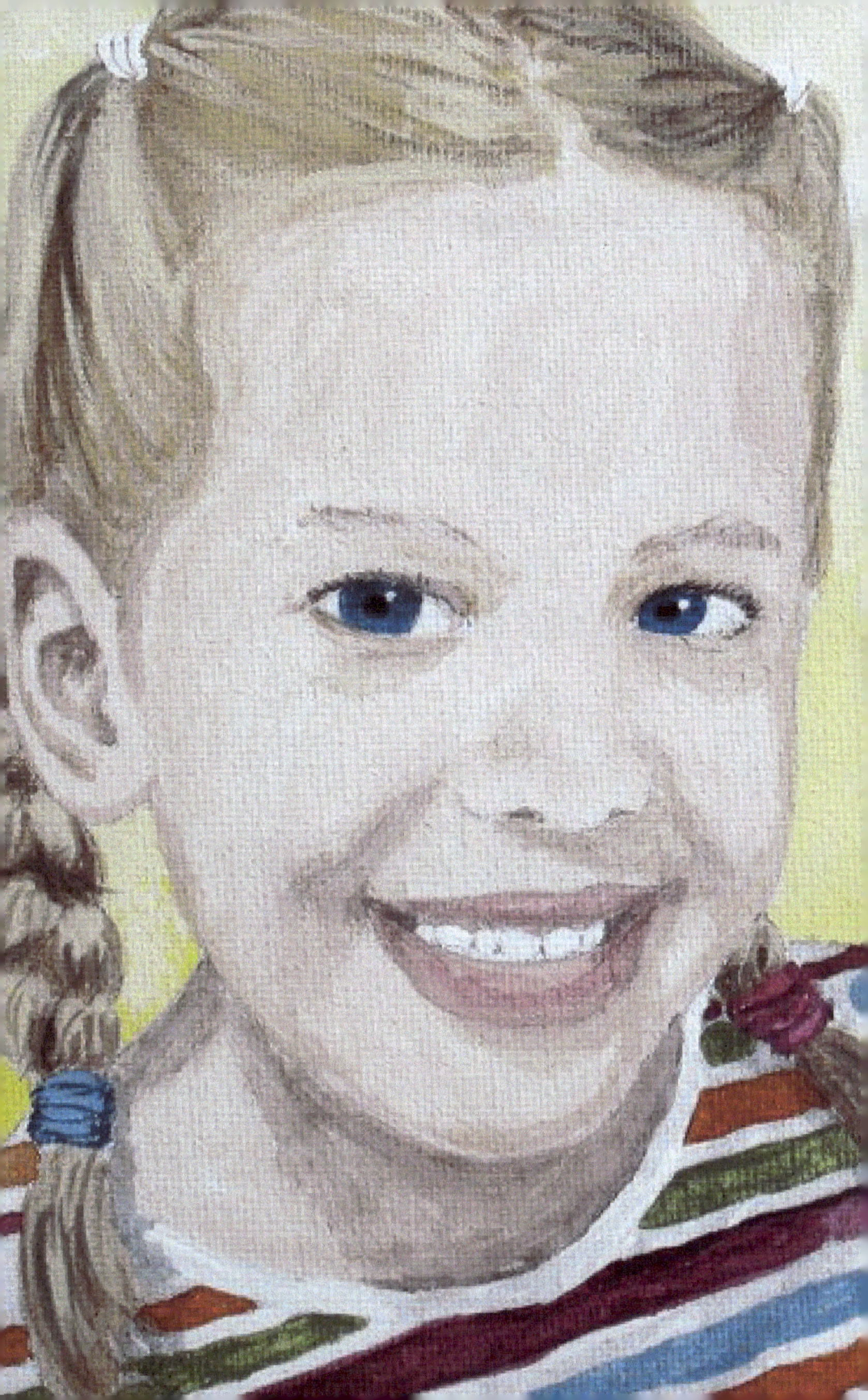

I won't let anyone look down on me!

I won't listen to the VOICES that tear me down.

I won't let anyone look down on me!

I will be an EXAMPLE in my life, my love, my faith.

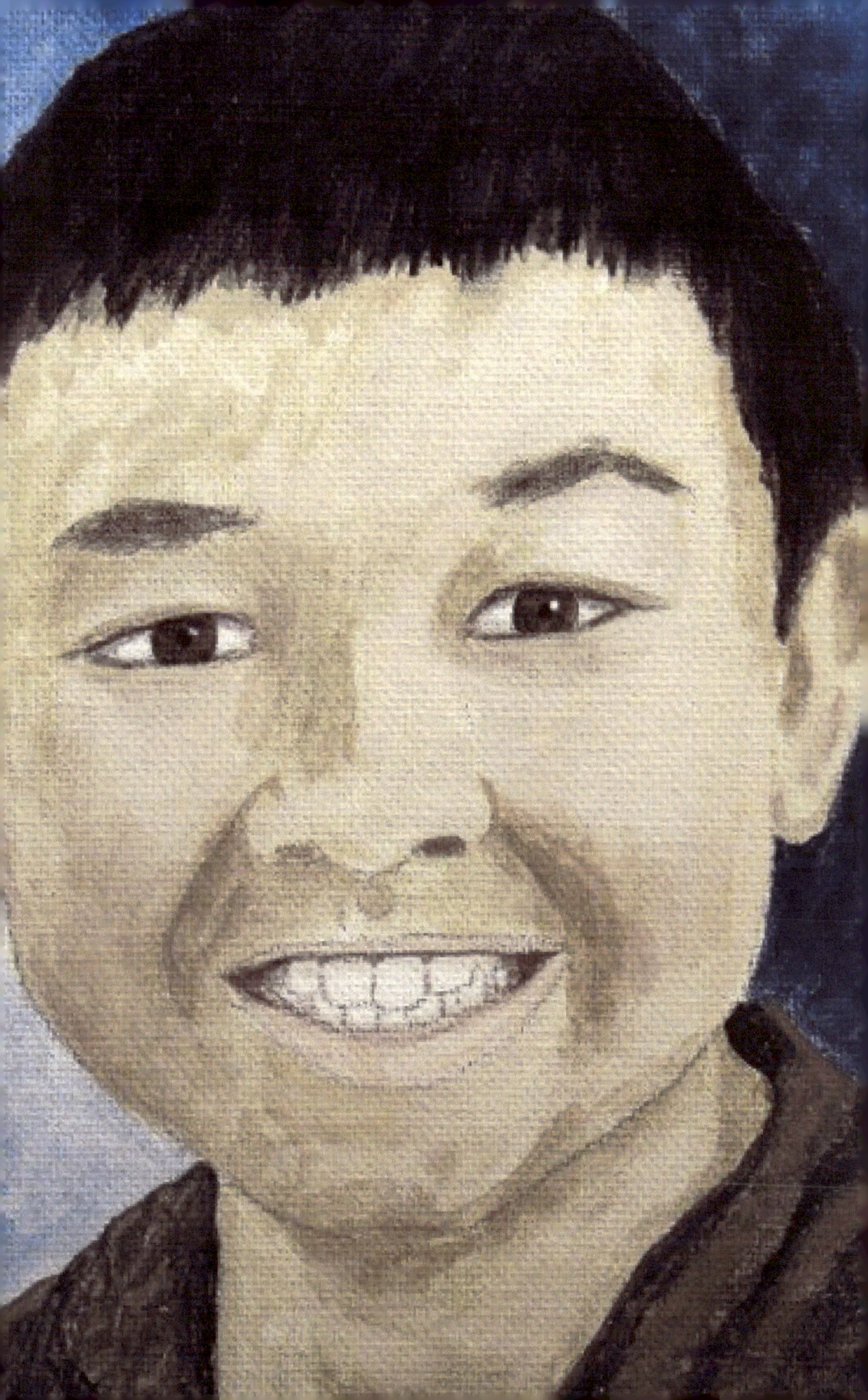

SOME SAY I am too young to understand.

Some say I haven't lived long enough to see.

But You as a child spoke the WORD in the temple.

And I know you can speak your word through me.

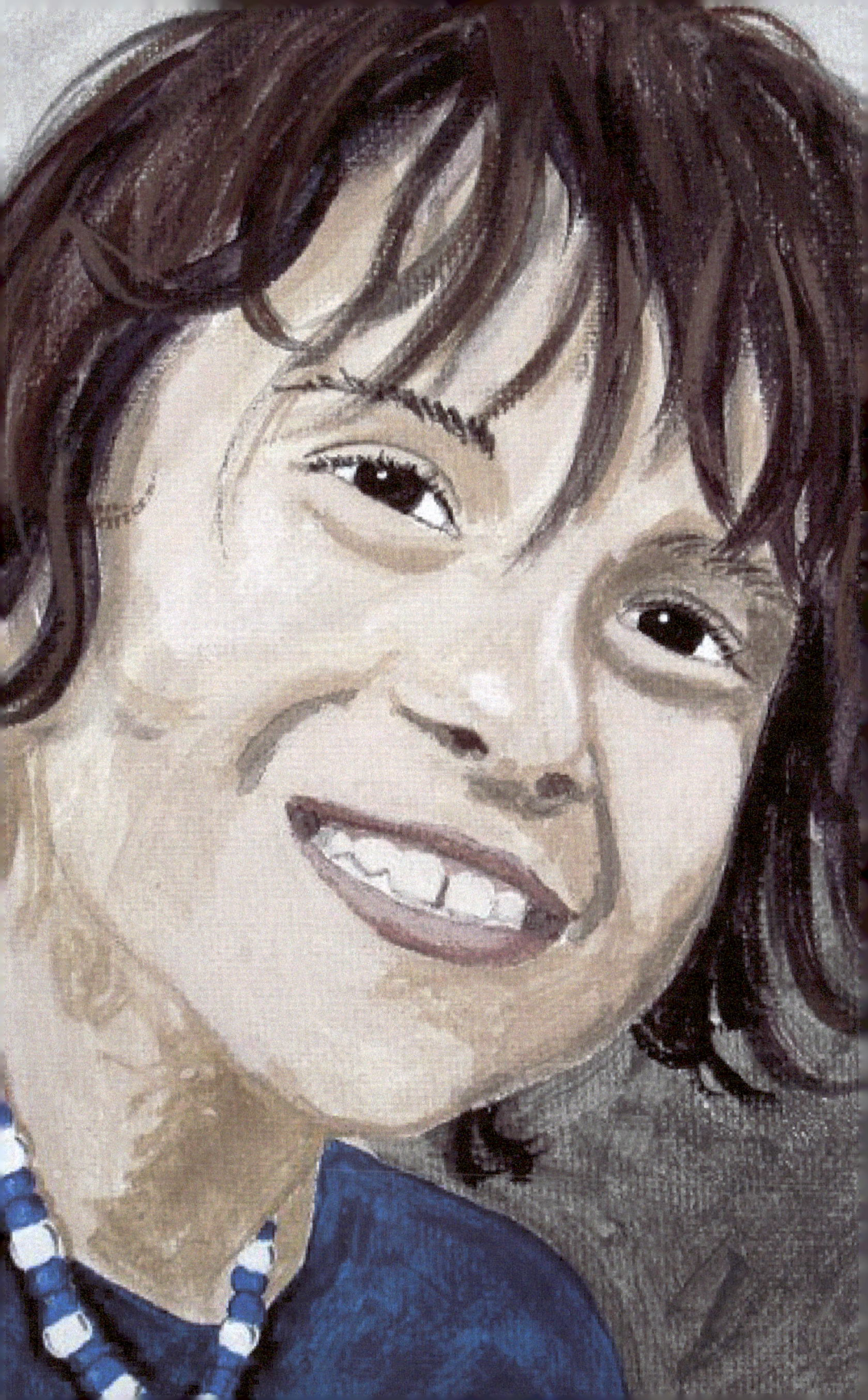

For God is using me.

Even in my youth, he's using me!

I will PERSEVERE, I will NOT GIVE UP,

for I know He has plans for me!

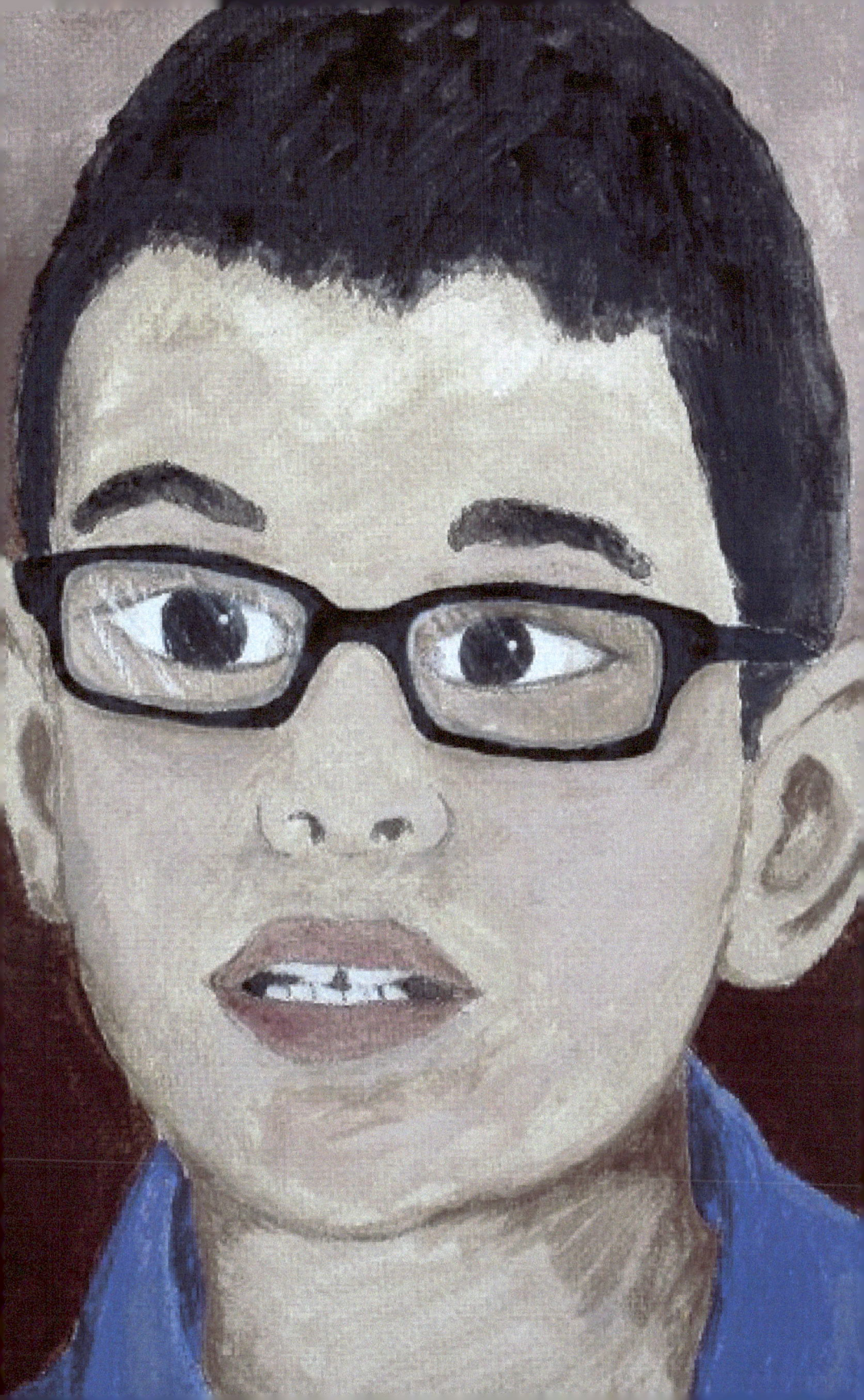

I'm SPECIAL!

I'm unique!

I am the one

God created me to be.

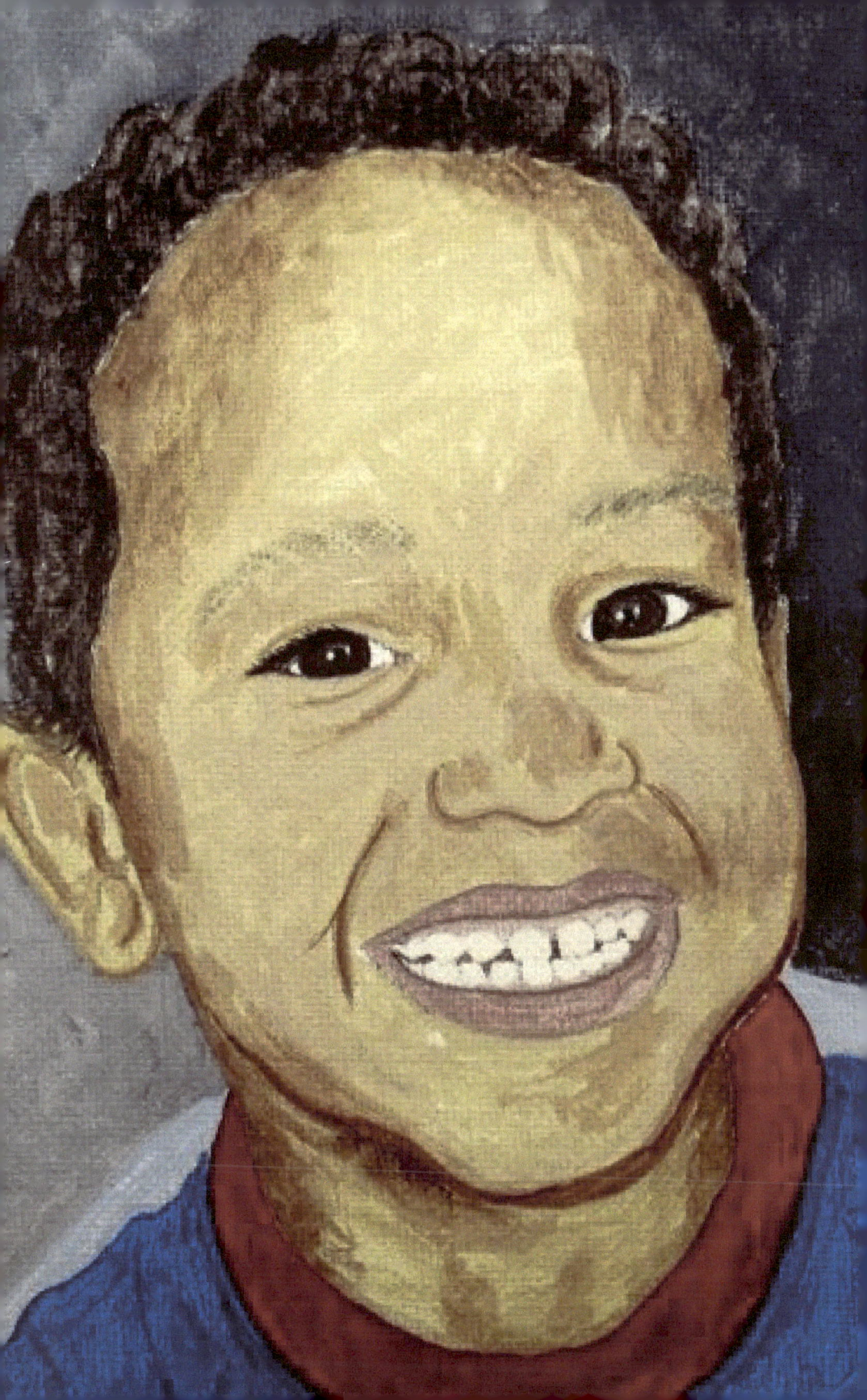

The GIFTS that I have,

the insight within,

make me different even from my best friend.

I'm special!

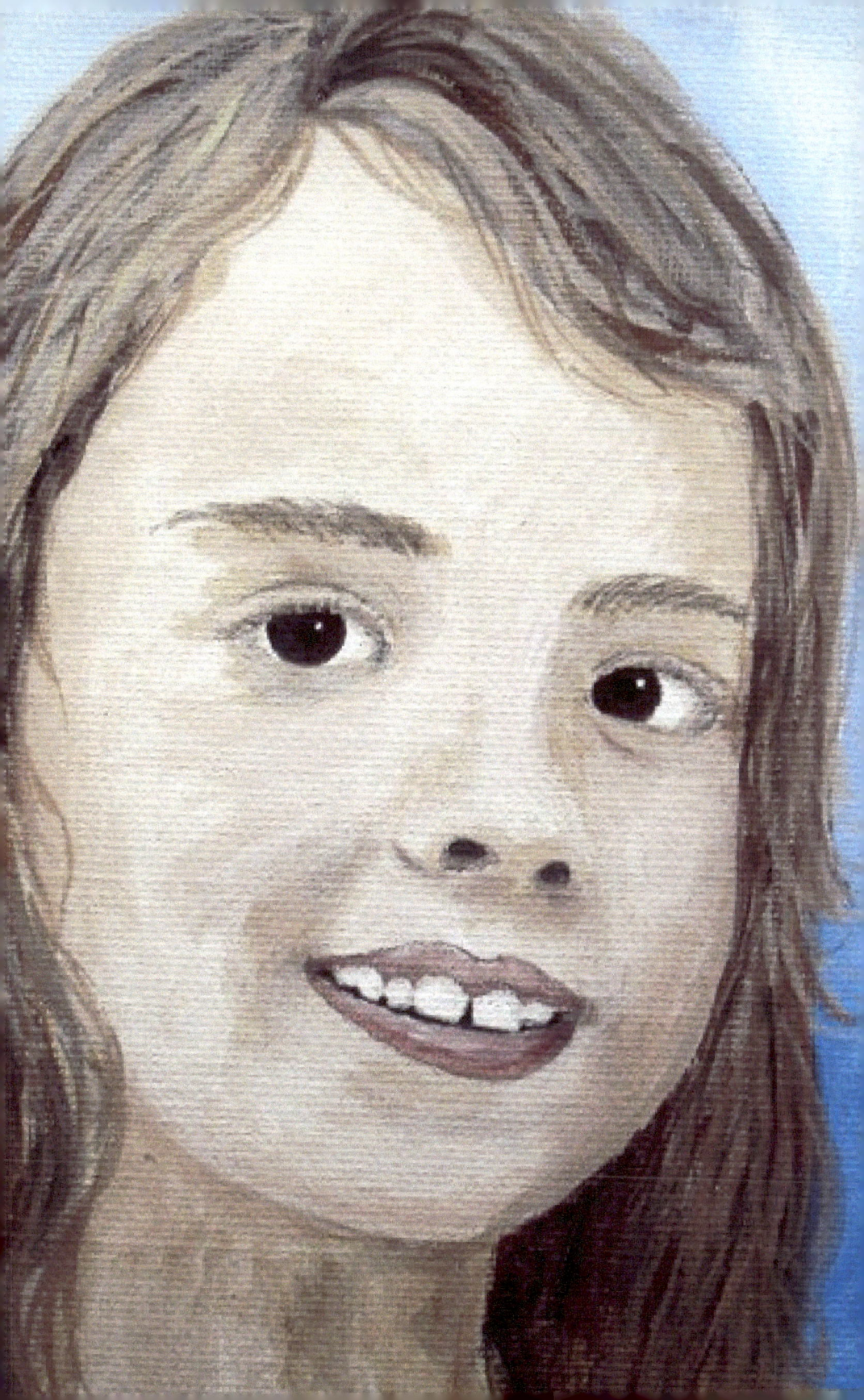

No matter what people say,

no matter what people do,

no matter how people feel,

I know you are the TRUTH.

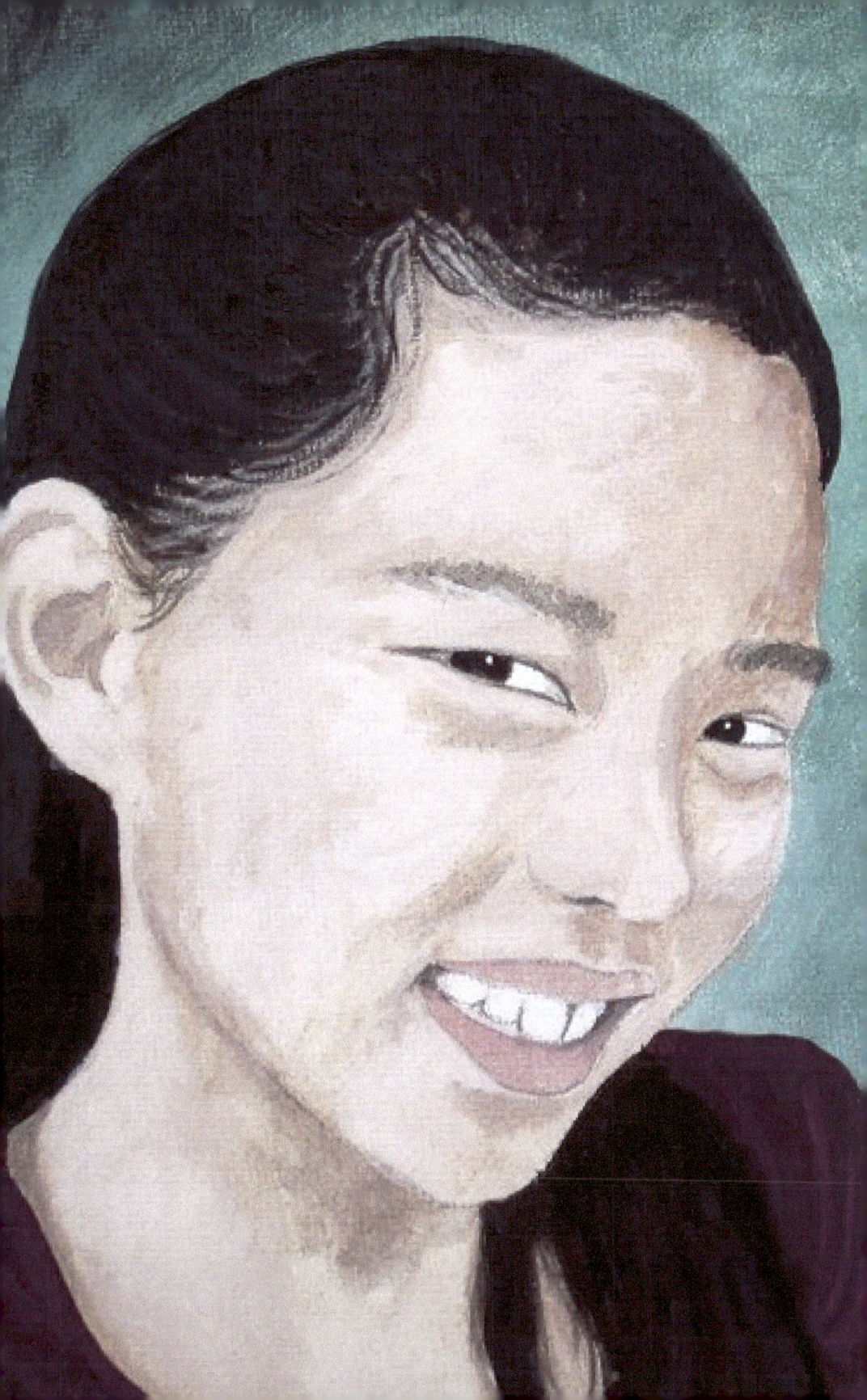

I gave my life to you.

I just want to be USED.

Whatever you have in store.

I know there's so much more!

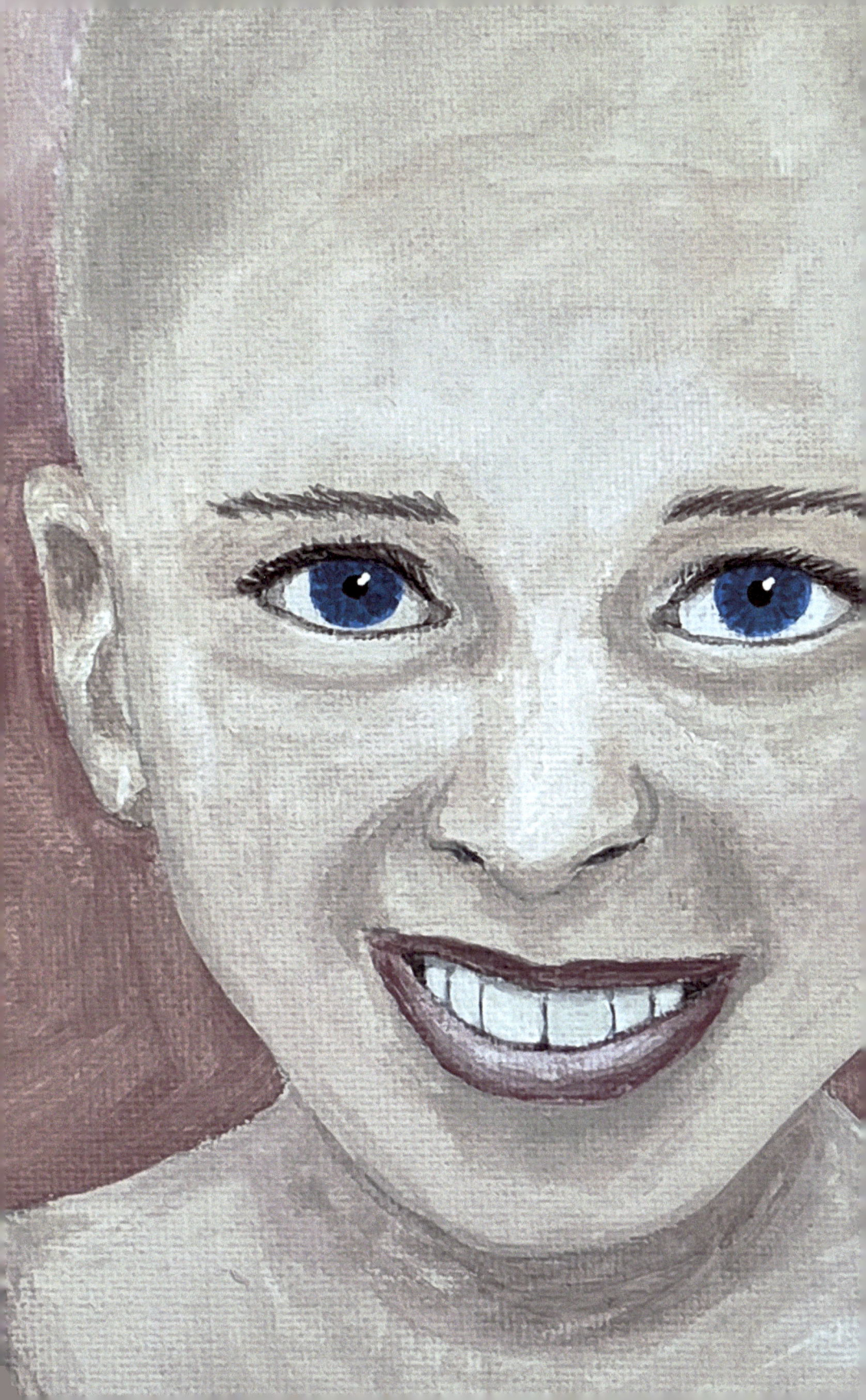

God, use my hands to lift you higher.

Use my VOICE to testify of your love.

Use my feet to dance before you.

In everything I do, I just want to be used.

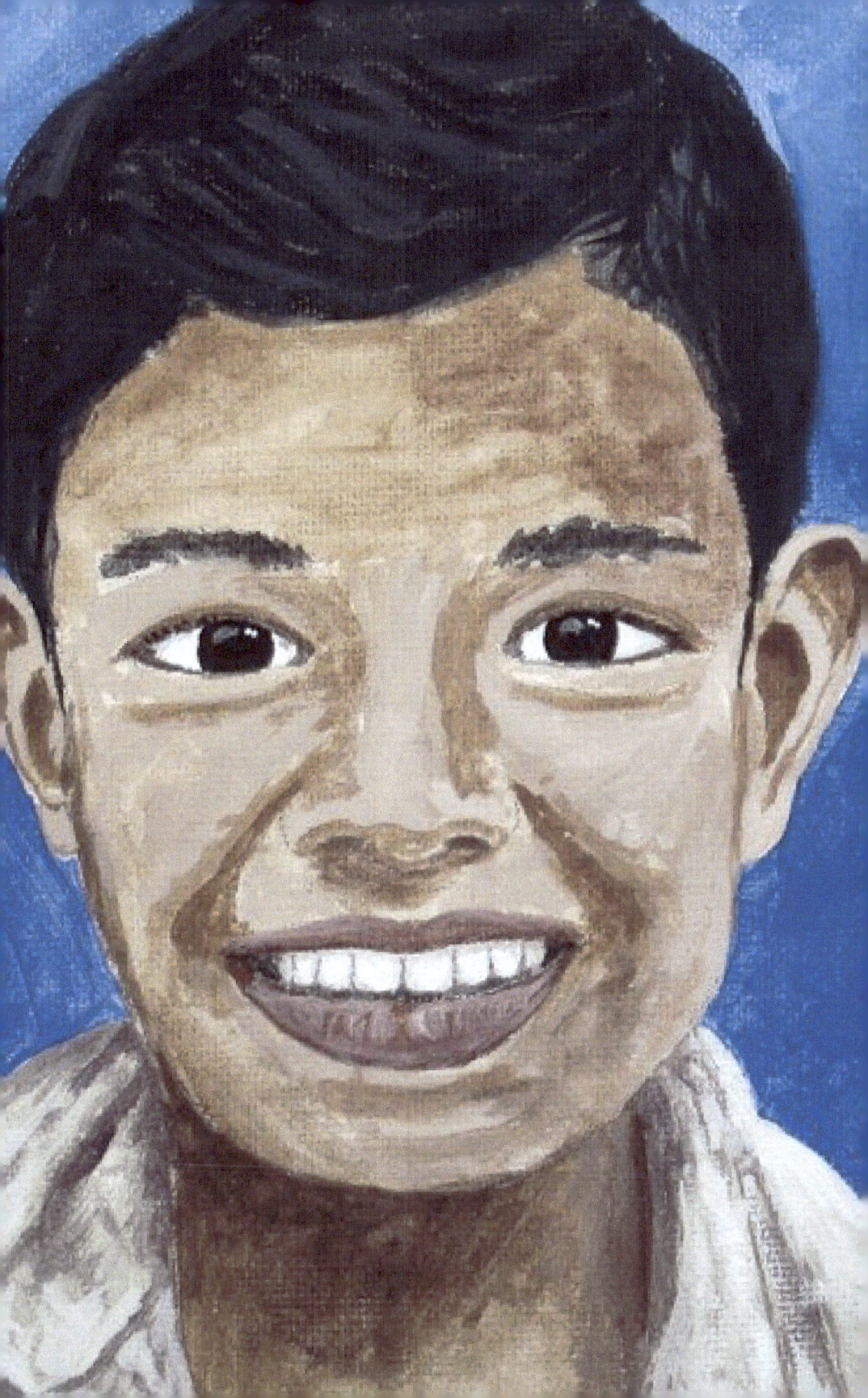

I do not have to be

like somebody else.

I know that I'm unique.

I can't be anyone but MYSELF!

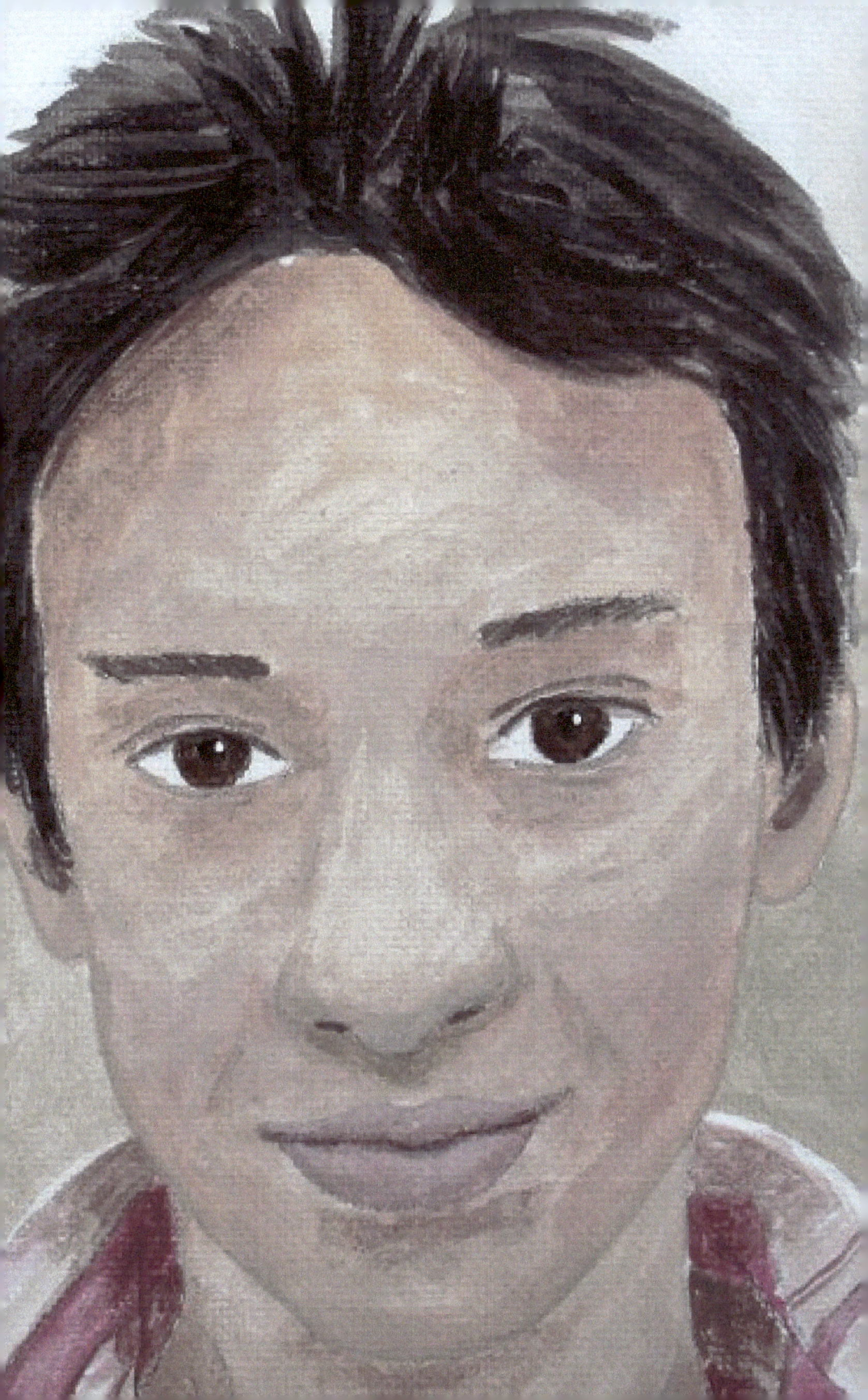

You have a special plan.

You know my destiny.

So as I TRUST in you,

I give myself as an offering.

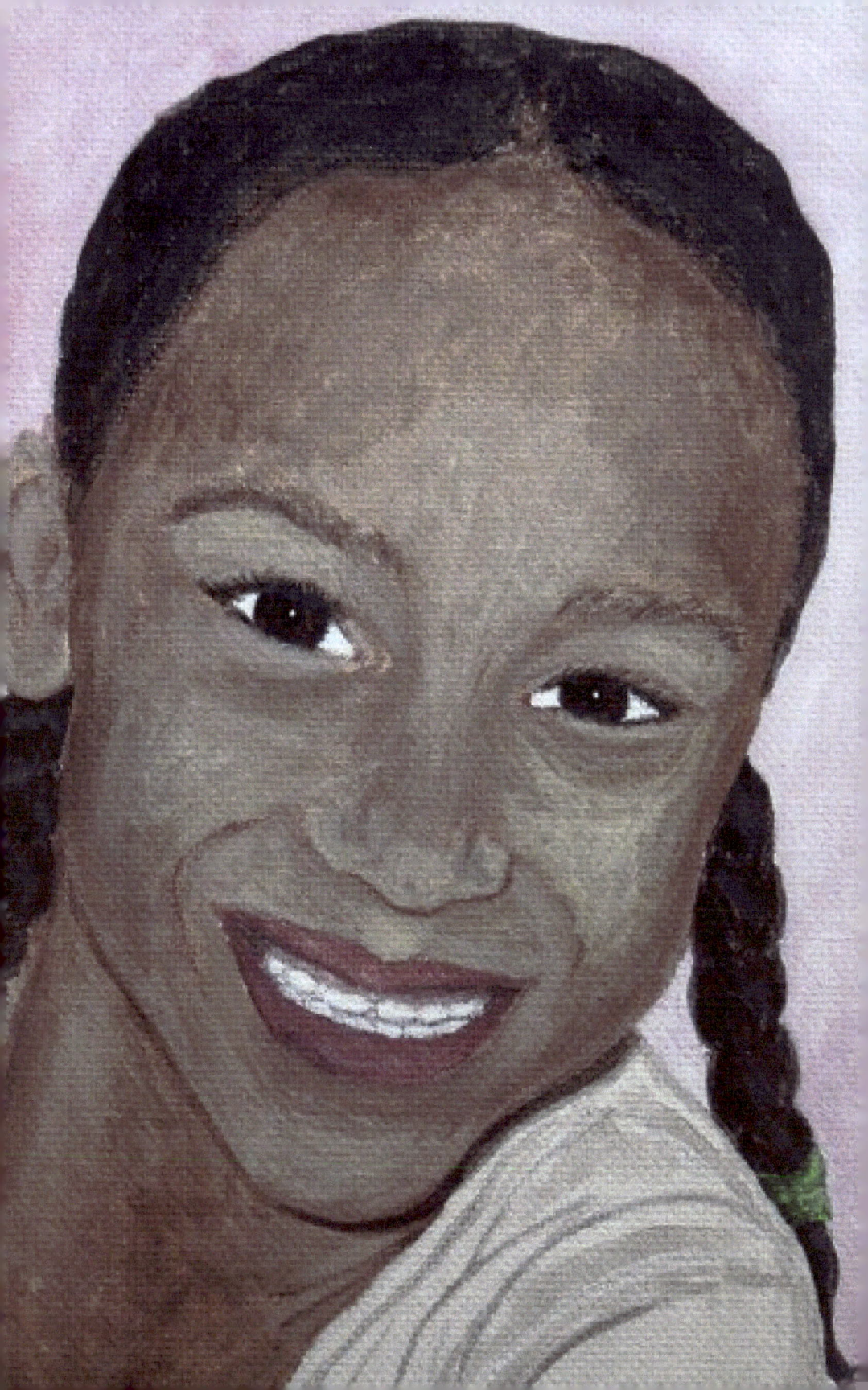

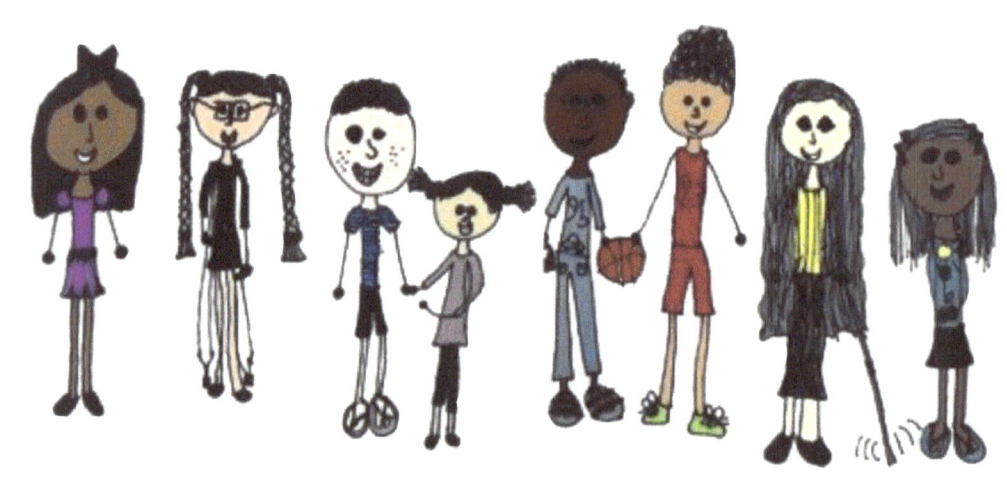

Selah, age 7, drew this with a sharpie and markers while we were recording *The Destiny Project* songs in the studio, capturing the diversity of the children of the world.

©2014 Selah Russell

I am
UNIQUE

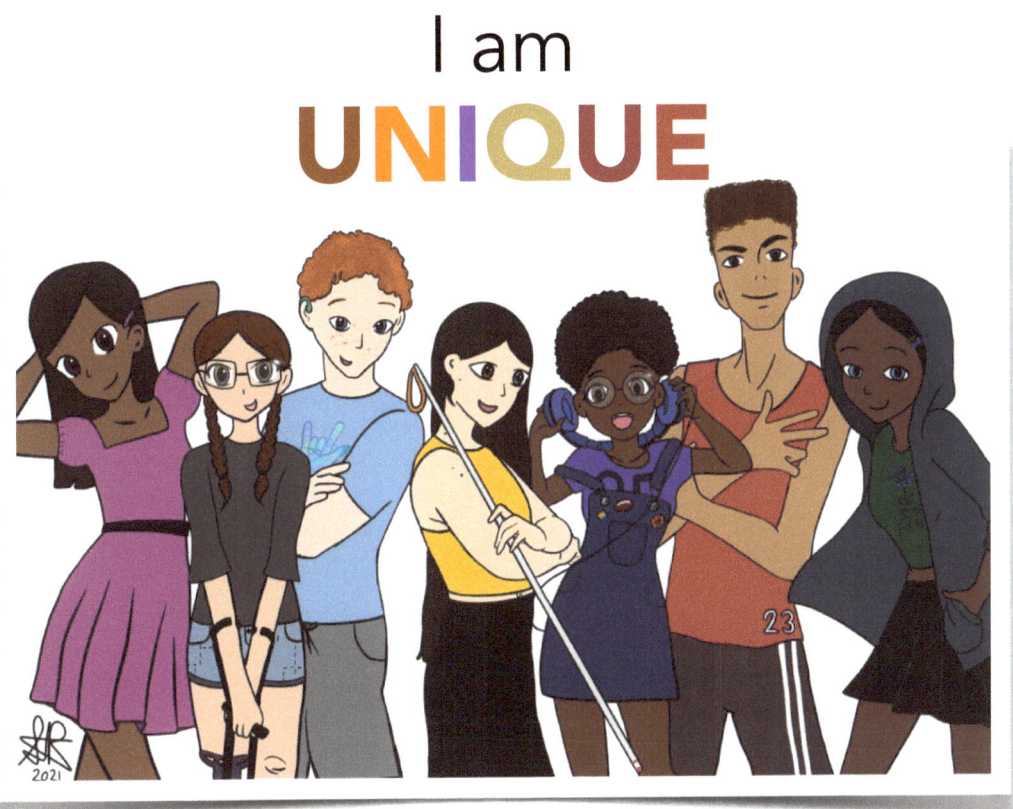

At age 16, Selah updated her drawing in ProCreate with stylized characters, continuing to include the uniqueness of each individual.

©2021 Selah Russell

VOCABULARY FOR DISCUSSION

The vocabulary words on the following page can be found in ALL CAPS in the same order as they appear on each of the book's pages.

Define them, read them in context of the songs, and discuss how they apply to you, your students, your family, and/or your children!

VOCABULARY FOR DISCUSSION

SIGNS
DETERMINED
PROSPER
DESIGNED
UNIQUE
CREATOR
WONDERFULLY MADE
DESTINY
PREVAIL
TOO YOUNG
VOICES
EXAMPLE
SOME SAY
PERSEVERE
NOT GIVE UP
SPECIAL
GIFTS
TRUTH
USED
VOICE
MYSELF
PLAN
TRUST

This project was made possible by the generous contributions from our Patrons. We are grateful for you!

Roman & Genevieve Ballock
A. Lois Barksdale
Arlene Barnard
Jessica Chanse
Rocklyn & Eva Clarke
Team DADKAH
Royal & Autumn Downs
Marya & Judson Flanagan
Louis & Sharon Froston
Josh, Cynthia & Rebekka Fulton
Michael & Lisa Gaskins
Margaret & Donald Granite
Paula R. Hudson
Bill & Linda Hughes
Donna & Terence Johns
Glen & Chih-Yi Kwok
Dominique Lafortune & Olivia Damas
Vanessa R. Martin
Semenya McCord
Zivai & April Mtyora
Sonja R. Naylor
Justin & Jessica Newry
The Payne Family
Annette Philip
Cynthia L. Russell
George & Sandra Russell
Howard Russell
Deborah & Jonathan Singleton
Alexander Thomas
Gideon & Yvonne Thompson
Matthew & Mona Thompson
Andrew & Courtney Ward
Brent & Jacquie Williams

Did you know that there are

SONGS

that go with this book?

All the words you are reading in this book are

lyrics to incredible songs

that will change your life!

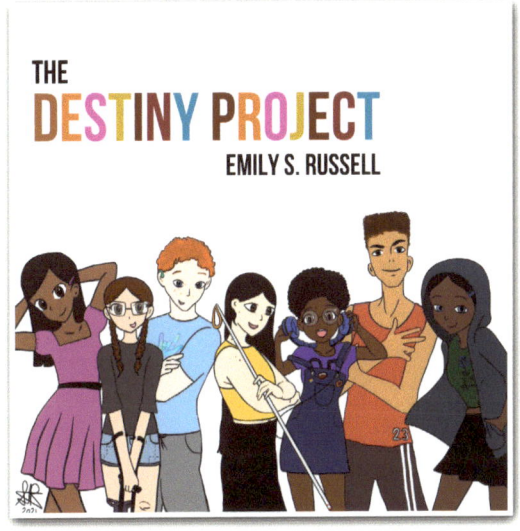

Download

THE DESTINY PROJECT

now on **Apple Music, Bandcamp,**

& most streaming platforms!

www.ingramcontent.com/pod-product-compliance
Lightning Source LLC
Chambersburg PA
CBHW040330220526
45473CB00009B/2637